Ladybug

Horned Beetle

Stinkbug

Stick Bug

This book is dedicated to my son, Jason, because of his appreciation for the small things in life, including bugs.

這本書要獻給我的兒子——Jason，因為他總能去欣賞生活中的微小事物，包括小蟲子。

Fleet's Sticky Feet

飛麗的黏腳丫

Grrrowl!

"My *tummy says it's lunch time," says Fleet the fly.

"Why don't you try to get some food from the picnic table?" Lily the ladybug says.

"Good idea!"

3

Fleet *lands on a big, blue bowl on the picnic table.
"Mmmm! Noodles!"

4

A hand *slaps at her. She tries to fly, but her feet *stick to the bowl.

"I'll help you, Fleet!" says Lily.

Lily pulls Fleet's feet free before the hand slaps again.

"Thanks, Lily," Fleet says.

"Your feet don't like to *let go, huh, Fleet."

"Yes, Lily. It *scares me when I get *stuck!"

A noodle falls to the ground.

"There's your lunch, Fleet!" Lily cries. "See you later!"

Fleet tastes the noodle.

10

But a foot *steps on it before she can eat.

"Whoah! That was too close!"

Grrrowl!

"I need to find something for my tummy," Fleet says.

She sees Bumpy the caterpillar sitting on a flower.

"Mmmm. Some flower juice would taste sweet."

14

She lands beside Bumpy.

"May I share the flower juice?" Fleet asks.

"Sure!" Bumpy says.

Fleet tries to drink but her feet stick to the flower *stem.

"Oh no!" Fleet cries. "My feet won't let go!"

"I'll help," Bumpy says.

17

Bumpy pulls Fleet free, but her feet stick to his body!

"Hey, let go!" Bumpy cries.

"I can't! My feet are stuck!"

19

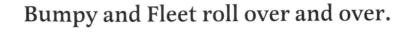
Bumpy and Fleet roll over and over.

They *bump into something hard.

Fleet's feet fly free of Bumpy's body.

"Oh no! What am I stuck to now?" Fleet cries.

"It's a bowl of *strawberry *jam," Bumpy says.

"Mmmmm. Lunch time!"

22

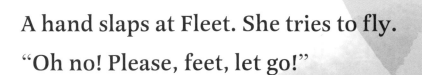

A hand slaps at Fleet. She tries to fly.

"Oh no! Please, feet, let go!"

"Clean the jam off your feet!" calls Macy the mantis.

Fleet cleans her feet and flies away just *in time.

"Mantises eat flies. Why would you help me?"

"A bit of grass is under my wing," Macy says. "I hope you'll take it out."

"I don't know—"

"I won't hurt you. I don't really like to eat flies."

"Well, okay."

Fleet lands on Macy's stomach and pulls out the grass.

"That feels good!" Macy says. "Now I have a *treat for you!"

"I hope it isn't *bug salad."

"Come and see!"

"Wow! Strawberry! I'm glad my feet stick to this!"

生字表

adj.=形ㄒㄧㄥˊ容ㄖㄨㄥˊ詞ㄘˊ，n.=名ㄇㄧㄥˊ詞ㄘˊ，v.=動ㄉㄨㄥˋ詞ㄘˊ

飛麗的黏腳丫

咕咕咕咕嚕！

蒼蠅飛麗說：「我的肚子說午餐時間到了。」

瓢蟲莉莉說：「為什麼不去那張野餐桌上拿點東西來吃呢？」

「好主意！」

飛麗停在野餐桌的一個藍色大碗上。

「嗯！是麵條耶！」

一隻手朝著她拍過來，飛麗想要飛走，但是她的腳卻緊黏在碗上。

莉莉說：「飛麗，我來幫妳！」

在那隻大手又拍過來之前，莉莉幫忙

拔起飛麗的腳。

飛麗說:「莉莉，謝啦！」

「妳的腳似乎不願意放開呢！是吧，飛麗?」

「是啊，莉莉。當我被黏住的時候，可真是嚇壞了！」

這時，有一條麵條掉在地上。

莉莉大叫:「飛麗，妳的午餐有著落了！那我走囉，再見！」

飛麗嚐了一口麵條，但在她還沒把它吃下去之前，就有一隻大腳把它一腳踩住。

「哇！真是好險啊！」

咕咕咕咕嚕！

飛麗說:「我得找點東西填

飽我的肚子才行。」

她看到毛毛蟲邦皮坐在一朵花上。

「嗯，花蜜嚐起來應該很甜吧！」

她在邦皮身旁停下來。

飛麗問:「你的花蜜可以分我一點嗎?」

邦皮說:「當然可以!」

飛麗想過去喝口花蜜，但是她的腳黏
在花梗上了。

飛麗大喊:「喔，不！我的腳又黏住了!」

邦皮說:「我來幫忙!」

邦皮將飛麗拉開，但是她的腳卻黏在
邦皮的身上了!

38

邦皮大喊:「喂！放開啦！」

「不行啦！我的腳黏住了！」

就這樣，邦皮和飛麗兩個一路滾著，直到撞上某個硬硬的東西後，飛麗的腳和邦皮的身體才分開。

飛麗大叫:「喔，不！現在我又黏到了什麼?」

邦皮說:「妳黏到了一碗草莓果醬。」

「嗯……看來午餐時間到了！」

一隻手又往飛麗拍過來。飛麗試著要飛走……

「喔，不！腳啊腳，
拜託你快點放開吧！」

這時，螳螂莓西大叫：「快把妳腳上的果醬弄乾淨！」

飛麗趕緊擦乾淨她的腳，然後及時飛走。

「螳螂是會吃蒼蠅的，妳為什麼要幫我啊？」

莓西說：「我的翅膀下卡著一些草，我希望妳能幫我拿出來。」

「嗯……我不確定……」

「我不會傷害妳的，我並不喜歡吃蒼蠅。」

「那好吧！」

飛麗飛到莓西的肚子上，然後把草拔出來。

莓西說:「感覺真舒服！現在讓我請妳一頓吧！」

「希望不是蟲蟲沙拉。」

「來看看就知道了嘛！」

「哇！草莓耶！真高興我的腳能黏在這顆草莓上！」

故事重組
Rearrange the story

在第 51 頁有 6 個句子，請把它們剪下，對照下面的圖片，並按照故事內容的發生順序，貼在虛線框框裡。

你³所ㄙㄨㄛ不ㄅㄨ知ㄓ的ㄉㄜ蒼ㄘㄤ蠅ㄧㄥ Fㄌㄧy

　　本ㄅㄣ書ㄕㄨ的ㄉㄜ主ㄓㄨ角ㄐㄩㄝ飛ㄈㄟ麗ㄌㄧ就ㄐㄧㄡ是ㄕ大ㄉㄚ家ㄐㄧㄚ熟ㄕㄡ知ㄓ的ㄉㄜ蒼ㄘㄤ蠅ㄧㄥ。蒼ㄘㄤ蠅ㄧㄥ一ㄧ生ㄕㄥ中ㄓㄨㄥ會ㄏㄨㄟ經ㄐㄧㄥ過ㄍㄨㄛ四ㄙ個ㄍㄜ階ㄐㄧㄝ段ㄉㄨㄢ：卵ㄌㄨㄢ、幼ㄧㄡ蟲ㄔㄨㄥ、蛹ㄩㄥ、成ㄔㄥ蟲ㄔㄨㄥ。在ㄗㄞ這ㄓㄜ些ㄒㄧㄝ階ㄐㄧㄝ段ㄉㄨㄢ中ㄓㄨㄥ，牠ㄊㄚ們ㄇㄣ的ㄉㄜ外ㄨㄞ表ㄅㄧㄠ都ㄉㄡ會ㄏㄨㄟ不ㄅㄨ一ㄧ樣ㄧㄤ，所ㄙㄨㄛ以ㄧ這ㄓㄜ個ㄍㄜ過ㄍㄨㄛ程ㄔㄥ叫ㄐㄧㄠ做ㄗㄨㄛ「完ㄨㄢ全ㄑㄩㄢ變ㄅㄧㄢ態ㄊㄞ」。除ㄔㄨ此ㄘ之ㄓ外ㄨㄞ，還ㄏㄞ有ㄧㄡ一ㄧ些ㄒㄧㄝ其ㄑㄧ他ㄊㄚ的ㄉㄜ昆ㄎㄨㄣ蟲ㄔㄨㄥ也ㄧㄝ會ㄏㄨㄟ經ㄐㄧㄥ歷ㄌㄧ「完ㄨㄢ全ㄑㄩㄢ變ㄅㄧㄢ態ㄊㄞ」的ㄉㄜ過ㄍㄨㄛ程ㄔㄥ，例ㄌㄧ如ㄖㄨ甲ㄐㄧㄚ蟲ㄔㄨㄥ、蝴ㄏㄨ蝶ㄉㄧㄝ、蜜ㄇㄧ蜂ㄈㄥ和ㄏㄜ螞ㄇㄚ蟻ㄧ等ㄉㄥ等ㄉㄥ。

　　蒼ㄘㄤ蠅ㄧㄥ每ㄇㄟ隻ㄓ腳ㄐㄧㄠ的ㄉㄜ前ㄑㄧㄢ端ㄉㄨㄢ都ㄉㄡ有ㄧㄡ個ㄍㄜ類ㄌㄟ似ㄙ吸ㄒㄧ盤ㄆㄢ的ㄉㄜ構ㄍㄡ造ㄗㄠ，使ㄕ牠ㄊㄚ們ㄇㄣ停ㄊㄧㄥ在ㄗㄞ光ㄍㄨㄤ滑ㄏㄨㄚ物ㄨ體ㄊㄧ的ㄉㄜ表ㄅㄧㄠ面ㄇㄧㄢ時ㄕ，不ㄅㄨ容ㄖㄨㄥ易ㄧ滑ㄏㄨㄚ

下來。牠們的嘴巴長得有點像大象的鼻子，是用來吸食液體食物的好幫手。

　　蒼蠅的眼睛是由四千個小眼構成的複眼，所以視線範圍比人類大，看的速度也比人類快。其他的昆蟲像蜻蜓和蝴蝶，也跟蒼蠅一樣擁有複眼，所以要接近牠們很不容易。而視力較差的螞蟻，複眼只包含一、兩百個小眼，所以牠們的反應也就沒有那麼快了。

關於作者

Kriss Erickson has been a freelance writer since 1981. She has published in the United States and in Australia and has over 300 published works. Kriss earned a Master's degree in Counseling in 2003 and holds a Master's level certificate of Spiritual Direction. She lives with her husband and son on a 3/4 acre wetland where she has created extensive gardens. Kriss is also a freelance artist in colored pencil and acrylic. She enjoys singing blues and contemporary music at local coffee shops.

Kriss Erickson 從 1981 年開始了自由作家的生活。她陸續在美國和澳洲發表著作，至今出版過的作品已超過 300 本。Kriss 在 2003 年取得心理諮商碩士的學位，並且擁有靈修指導碩士程度的結業證書。她和丈夫以及兒子住在四分之三英畝的濕地上，還在那裡打造了一個廣闊的花園。Kriss 同時也是一位自由藝術家，擅長使用色鉛筆和壓克力顏料來畫畫，而在當地的咖啡店哼唱藍調和現代音樂則是她的樂趣。

關於繪者

陽光，綠蔭，
花和青草味，
樹影和月光，蛙鳴。
童年的盛夏。

一個透明的玻璃瓶，瓶口用橡皮筋箍著紙蓋，上面扎有幾個氣孔，將裡面裝滿大大小小的、知名的或是不知名的蟲兒，然後安靜而好奇的看上好長一陣子，這是整個季節裡最興趣盎然的事情之一了。許多歲以後，複雜、莫名的東西多起來，心中不再有那個帶紙蓋的瓶子，不再關心、甚至不再靜心聆聽周圍的一切。

身為卡圖工作室的一份子，畫畫、做書，我們努力為孩子們製造著快樂，同樣也為自己尋找單純和美好。

親親自然 成就英語悅讀

台北市外語啟蒙教學發展學會理事長　　李宗玥

「故事」是每個孩子的夢工廠，成就孩子的豐富幻想，讓孩子的想像力無限伸展與飛翔，每個故事都在架構成長的快樂回憶，細數故事的數目，如同細數快樂。

「自然世界」是兒童生活經驗中，最真實與迷人的經驗。不起眼的毛毛蟲為什麼會變成一隻漂漂亮亮的蝴蝶？自然世界裡充滿了讓孩子忍不住驚喜的讚嘆，如同作者的孩子，琢磨於生活中的微小事物，一隻小蟲子也能成就一個大驚奇，從孩子的眼裡視察自然，會發現自然世界本身就是一個故事屋。

「語言」是迎向世界最萬能的鑰匙，它開啟每一扇快樂夢想的門；而每一扇門後，有著世界各個角落裡孩子的喜悅與幻想。有了語言的鑰匙，才有機會透視世界更多的快樂夢想，才有機會了解故事裡的昆蟲們，是如何相處互動的。

三民書局的「我的昆蟲朋友」系列，用「語言」的骨架，串連了「故事」與「自然世界」，搭起孩子閱讀的興趣與動機，讓「語言」(language) 與「知識」(knowledge) 不再毫無交集、枯燥乏味。就是這樣的書，會讓我們和孩子都感動。任何一種有目的的學習，在學習歷程中，都會有高低潮，我相信藉著「我的昆蟲朋友」系列中有趣的自然故事與好玩的學習活動，必然能逐步架構語言的樂趣與能力。

　　語言的學習，早就應擺脫制式語言文法架構，而走入孩子的真實生活裡。如果您也有同樣的想法，相信在「昆蟲朋友」的「自然世界」中，必能滿足您對孩子語言發展的夢想與期盼。

BUG BUDDIES SERIES 我的昆蟲朋友系列

具基礎英文閱讀能力者（國小 4～6 年級適讀）

我有幾個昆蟲好朋友，各個都有自己奇怪的特性，讓他們有點煩惱；可是這樣的不同，卻帶給他們意想不到的驚奇與結果！

「我的昆蟲朋友」共有五個：

1. Bumpy's Crazy Tail 　　邦皮的瘋狂尾巴
2. Fleet's Sticky Feet 　　飛麗的黏腳丫
3. Stilt's Stick Problem 　史提的大麻煩
4. Macy's Strange Snacks　莓西的怪點心
5. Stinky's Funny Scent 　丁奇的怪味道

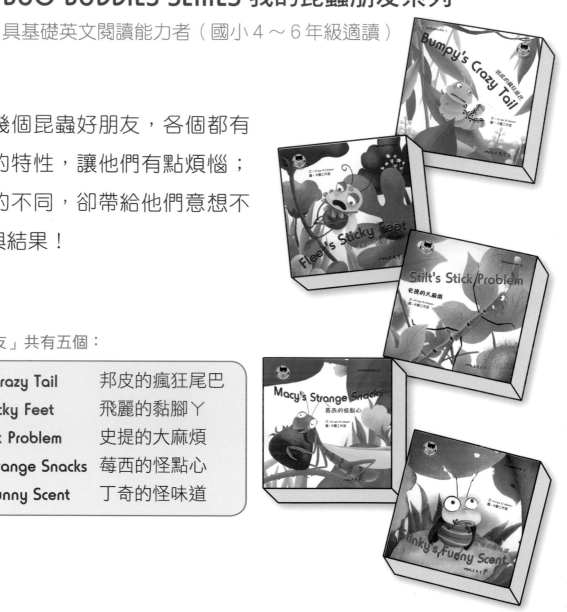

Fleet helps Macy to pull out the grass under her wing.	Fleet's feet fly free of Bumpy's body, but stick to a bowl of strawberry jam.
Macy tells Fleet to clean her feet and Fleet could fly away.	Fleet's feet stick to the bowl on the picnic table.
Macy has a strawberry treat for Fleet.	Fleet drinks the flower juice with Bumpy, but her feet stick to Bumpy's body.

- 故事重組解答

1. Fleet's feet stick to the bowl on the picnic table.
2. Fleet drinks the flower juice with Bumpy, but her feet stick to Bumpy's body.
3. Fleet's feet fly free of Bumpy's body, but stick to a bowl of strawberry jam.
4. Macy tells Fleet to clean her feet and Fleet could fly away.
5. Fleet helps Macy to pull out the grass under her wing.
6. Macy has a strawberry treat for Fleet.

國家圖書館出版品預行編目資料

Fleet's Sticky Feet:飛麗的黏腳丫 / Kriss Erickson
著;卡圖工作室繪;本局編輯部譯.－－初版一刷.
－－臺北市：三民，2006
　　面；　公分.－－(Fun心讀雙語叢書.我的昆蟲
朋友系列)
中英對照
ISBN 957－14－4596－7　　(精裝)

1. 英國語言－讀本

523.38　　　　　　　　　　　　　95014837

© 　Fleet's Sticky Feet
　　　──飛麗的黏腳丫

著作人　Kriss Erickson
繪　者　卡圖工作室
譯　者　本局編輯部
發行人　劉振強
著作財
產權人　三民書局股份有限公司
　　　　臺北市復興北路386號
發行所　三民書局股份有限公司
　　　　地址／臺北市復興北路386號
　　　　電話／(02)25006600
　　　　郵撥／0009998－5
印刷所　三民書局股份有限公司
門市部　復北店／臺北市復興北路386號
　　　　重南店／臺北市重慶南路一段61號
初版一刷　2006年8月
編　號　S 806741
定　價　新臺幣參佰元整
行政院新聞局登記證局版臺業字第○二○○號

http://www.sanmin.com.tw　三民網路書店